Hair

Written by Pete Jenkins
Illustrated by Hazel Quintanilla

Rourke
Educational Media
rourkeeducationalmedia.com

Before & After Reading Activities

Teaching Focus:

Teacher-child conversations: Teacher-child conversations play an important role in shaping what children learn. Practice this and see how these conversations help scaffold your student's learning.

Before Reading:

Building Academic Vocabulary and Background Knowledge

Before reading a book, it is important to set the stage for your child or student by using pre-reading strategies. This will help them develop their vocabulary, increase their reading comprehension, and make connections across the curriculum.

1. Read the title and look at the cover. *Let's make predictions about what this book will be about.*
2. Take a picture walk by talking about the pictures/photographs in the book. Implant the vocabulary as you take the picture walk. Be sure to talk about the text features such as headings, the Table of Contents, glossary, bolded words, captions, charts/ diagrams, or Index.
3. Have students read the first page of text with you then have students read the remaining text.
4. Strategy Talk – use to assist students while reading.
   - Get your mouth ready
   - Look at the picture
   - Think…does it make sense
   - Think…does it look right
   - Think…does it sound right
   - Chunk it – by looking for a part you know
5. Read it again.

Content Area Vocabulary
Use glossary words in a sentence.

cap
curly
grows
hair

After Reading:

Comprehension and Extension Activity

After reading the book, work on the following questions with your child or students in order to check their level of reading comprehension and content mastery.

1. *Do you have hair anywhere on your body besides your head? (Summarize)*
2. *Why do you think everyone's hair is different? (Asking Questions)*
3. *Why does your hair need to be washed and brushed? (Text to self connection)*
4. *What makes your hair special? (Asking Questions)*

Extension Activity

Look around your classroom or home. What kinds of hair do your classmates or family have? Are they the same color, length, texture? On a piece of construction paper, draw a picture of your friends or family with their hair. How are they different? How are they the same?

Table of Contents

Everyone's Hair
is Different.................... 4

I Have to Wash
My Hair? 12

Hair Grows 16

Picture Glossary........... 23

About the Author 24

Everyone's Hair is Different

I see my **hair**.
It's on my head.

5

I saw Maria's hair.

It looks funny when she gets out of bed.

I see my hair.

It is brown and curly.

I saw Caleb's hair.

It is long and swirly.

I Have to Wash My Hair?

I see my hair.

I wash it every day.

I saw Kimo's hair.

She pulls it back
when we play.

Hair Grows

I see my hair. It **grows** and grows.

17

I saw Jack's hair.

He wears a **cap** so it
barely shows.

I see my hair.

It is part of me.

I love my hair!

Picture Glossary

 **cap** (kap): A soft, flat hat, sometimes with a visor in the front.

 **curly** (KUR-lee): When your hair is curly, it is twisted and swirly.

 **grows** (grohs): When your hair grows, it gets longer.

 **hair** (hair): The thin, soft strands that grow from your head.

About the Author

Pete Jenkins loves to write books for children. He also likes to travel, read, and he is often seen combing his hair and trying different things with it. He likes to be different and thinks your hair is just one way you can express yourself!

Meet The Author!
www.meetREMauthors.com

Library of Congress PCN Data

Hair/ Pete Jenkins
(I See, I Saw)
ISBN 978-1-68342-311-9 (hard cover)
ISBN 978-1-68342-407-9 (soft cover)
ISBN 978-1-68342-477-2 (e-Book)
Library of Congress Control Number: 2017931161

Rourke Educational Media
Printed in the United States of America,
North Mankato, Minnesota

www.rourkeeducationalmedia.com

Edited by: Keli Sipperley
Cover and interior illustrations by: Hazel Quintanilla
Page layout by: Kathy Walsh